1314

920
STO

Stone, Melissa

You don't own me!

$14.64

DATE		
NOV 30 1992		
DEC 6 1992		
DEC 14 1992		
MAR 23 1993		
MAR 30 1993		

920
STO

You don't own me!

1314

BAKER & TAYLOR BOOKS

You Don't Own Me!

Program Consultants

Stephanie Abraham Hirsh, Ph.D.
Associate Director
National Staff Development Council
Dallas, Texas

Louise Matteoni, Ph.D.
Professor of Education
Brooklyn College
City University of New York

Karen Tindel Wiggins
Social Studies Consultant
Richardson Independent School District
Richardson, Texas

Renee Levitt
Educational Consultant
Scarsdale, New York

 **Steck-Vaughn Company**

A Subsidiary of National Education Corporation

MOMENTS IN AMERICAN HISTORY

You Don't Own Me!

BY
Melissa Stone

STECK-VAUGHN
LITERATURE LIBRARY

Steck-Vaughn Literature Library
Moments in American History

RISKING IT ALL
REBELLION'S SONG
CREATIVE DAYS
RACING TO THE WEST
YOU DON'T OWN ME!
CLOUDS OF WAR
A CRY FOR ACTION
LARGER THAN LIFE
FLYING HIGH
BRIGHTER TOMORROWS

Illustrations: Floyd Cooper: cover art, pp. 8-9, 11, 12, 15, 16, 19; Lyle Miller: pp. 20-21, 22, 25, 26, 28-29, 31; Linda Graves: pp. 32-33, 35, 37, 38-39, 41, 43; Arvis Stewart: pp. 44-45, 47, 48, 50, 53, 55; Ron Himler: pp. 56-57, 58, 61, 62, 65, 67; Christa Kieffer: pp. 68-69, 71, 73, 75, 77, 79.

Project Editor: Anne Souby

Design: Kirchoff/Wohlberg, Inc.

ISBN 0-8114-4079-6 (pbk.)
ISBN 0-8114-2669-6 (lib. bdg.)   LC 89-110885

CONTENTS

1825

ELIZABETH CADY STANTON ►
This wife and mother
shocked her community
by demanding the vote
for women.
(1826-1848)

◄ **ANGELINA
AND SARAH GRIMKÉ**
Two sisters from the South
followed their consciences
and spoke out against slavery.
(1829-1838)

LORENZO DE ZAVALA ►
An experienced Mexican
politician helped found
the Republic of Texas.
(1835-1836)

WILLIAM TRAVIS ➤
This leader and his brave men fought to the death to win independence for Texas. (1836)

◄ **WILLIAM AND ELLEN CRAFT**
To win their freedom, this slave couple became convincing actors. (1848)

HARRIET TUBMAN ➤
She operated an Underground Railroad, taking slaves on a fast track to freedom. (1856)

Harriet Tubman

A Conductor on the Underground Railroad

I was born a slave. I was beaten, abused, made to work long hours in the hot sun. One day I was even hit on the head with a two-pound weight.

But I escaped. And now I help other slaves escape to freedom. It is difficult work. It requires courage and daring. But it is a success!

A twig snapped. The three runaway slaves huddled in the shadows. They didn't dare move, didn't dare talk, didn't dare whisper or even swallow. They knew that the slightest noise might give them away.

The three friends — John, Eliza, and Henry — had run away from the plantation several hours earlier. Now they listened for the sounds of a search party. They tried to be brave, but the thought of being caught made them shudder. They knew what happened to slaves who tried to escape. They were punished as an example for other slaves. Most were whipped, but some were branded with hot irons.

As the three waited, they grew more and more frightened. Every noise made them jump. The hooting of an owl, the rustling of leaves — any sound at all might signal trouble.

Suddenly, someone stepped out of the bushes and stood before them. Panic rose in their throats. But the person raised her hand in a peaceful greeting.

"It's me. Time to go north."

That was all she said. The runaways knew instantly that it was Harriet Tubman, a black woman who had run away from her own master six years ago. The slaves called her "Moses." Like

Moses in the Bible, she had come to lead her people to freedom.

On this night in November 1856, Harriet directed the three runaways to follow her through the dense woods.

"We have to hurry," she whispered. "We have to make it to the first stop on the Railroad by morning."

John, Eliza, and Henry all nodded silently. They knew what she meant. She was talking about the Underground Railroad, which really wasn't a railroad at all. It was a series of escape routes for slaves. The routes led to northern states where slavery did not exist. People who were part of the Railroad provided runaways with food and shelter along the way to freedom.

"Do you think our master will have a big search party out looking for us?" Eliza whispered as she followed close behind Harriet.

"Oh, he'll have more than one," Harriet said grimly.

"More than one? But why?" Eliza asked nervously. "The last time some people tried to escape from Master Harrington, he only sent out a small group to find them."

Harriet stopped and turned to face the three runaways.

"Think about it," she said. "John here is a head slave. He's an overseer. He's more valuable to your master than ten ordinary slaves. Besides, since John is so important, they don't like for him

12

to set a bad example. They think it will encourage other slaves to run away. I bet that your master will have many slave hunters on our trail."

AS Harriet spoke, she saw terror creep over the faces of the three runaways. Softening her voice, she added a few reassuring words.

"Now don't you worry," she said. "I've made a dozen trips over this Railroad. I'm the most experienced conductor alive. And I'll tell you something: I've never lost a single passenger, and I don't intend to lose one now."

With that, she turned and made her way through the woods. After a while she led her passengers out to the main road.

"This is the most dangerous way to go," she told them, "but it's also the fastest. So keep your ears open. If you hear anyone coming — if you hear anything at all — run into the woods."

With their hearts pounding, they hurried down the road. Luck was with them, for there were no other travelers out that night. As morning dawned, however, a strange feeling came over Harriet.

"Something's wrong!" she hissed. "There's trouble up ahead. I can feel it."

Instantly she signaled to John, Eliza, and Henry to follow her into the woods.

"What did you see?" Eliza whispered breathlessly.

"I didn't see anything. But I felt something. I just know there's trouble. I don't mean to frighten you, but there's no time to waste. If your master is using bloodhounds to track us, they could catch up to us any minute. We must find a river or a stream. That's the only way to get the dogs off our trail. Dogs can't follow our scent in water."

Then Harriet was off again, darting through the trees. She kept racing full-speed ahead. When Henry begged to stop and catch his breath, she shook her head. There was no time to rest. They had to hurry.

Harriet was worried now. Every muscle in her body ached as she pushed through the underbrush. She was not on a familiar trail. She didn't know how to get to the first station from here.

"I can't let them know I'm afraid," she told herself. "They're counting on me. If they panic, we'll never make it." She said a silent prayer and kept moving. Gradually, she regained her courage.

AT last the group came to a river. Harriet told her three passengers to follow her across. Henry agreed, but John and Eliza protested.

"The river's too deep," Eliza stammered.

"We'll drown if we try to cross this river," John

pleaded. "We don't know how to swim. Why, we'd be better off facing Master Harrington than trying to cross this river."

Harriet looked at John with sadness and frustration. She had seen this happen before. Runaways sometimes became paralyzed with fear and weakened by hunger and lack of sleep. In a moment of despair, they decided it would be easier to turn back. But Harriet couldn't let this happen. She knew that returning slaves would be tortured until they revealed the secrets of the Underground Railroad. Then everyone working with the runaways would be in danger. She had to save the Railroad at all costs.

Silently she pulled out her gun and pointed it directly at John.

She said menacingly, "The choice is yours. Go with me or die."

One look at her face told John that she was serious. Frightened, he slid down the riverbank and began wading through the water. Eliza and Henry followed him. As Harriet plunged in behind them, she hoped that the river would not be too deep. Soon the water came up to their waists, then to their shoulders. Harriet, who was only five feet two inches tall, had water lapping at her chin. Finally, they made it across.

FROM here, Harriet trusted her instincts to lead her to the first station. After another desperate hour of traveling, she saw the woods thin out and a small settlement up ahead.

"There's the first station," she whispered to her passengers. "That house right over there." She pointed to a modest house at the edge of a clearing.

She crept up to the back door and knocked softly.

"Who is it?" came a voice from behind the door.

"A friend with friends," Harriet replied.

That was the signal. The door opened, and a tall man motioned for her to bring the runaways inside. The man gave them food, dry clothes, and a place to rest. When evening came, Harriet thanked him, then led her passengers back out into the woods. Traveling at night provided some safety for them.

To get back to the road, Harriet and her passengers retraced their steps. Once again they had to wade across the river. When they reached the main road, they saw that a search party had indeed been after them.

"Look," Harriet said, "see these cigar butts and this trampled grass? That's where they waited while their dogs were tracking us."

"Moses," said John in awe, "if you hadn't forced us to cross that river, we surely would have been caught."

Harriet knew that John was trying to apologize for his behavior at the river.

"The only thing that matters is that we *weren't* caught," she said gently. "Now let's get going."

As they continued down the road, Eliza spotted a poster nailed to a tree. She didn't know how to read, but John did.

"This is a 'Wanted' poster," he exclaimed. "Master Harrington is offering a $2,600 reward for our capture. And there's a $12,000 reward for the capture of Moses, the leader of the Underground Railroad."

Harriet laughed. "No one is going to catch me, no matter how much money they offer."

Over the next several days, Harriet took John, Eliza, and Henry to a series of stations. Some were the homes of Quakers. Other homes belonged to German immigrants or free blacks. The runaways hid behind false walls and underneath trapdoors during the day. Then, when night came, they were off again, always heading north.

At last, Harriet and her passengers made it to Philadelphia, a free city in Pennsylvania. They did not stop there long, however.

"Slaveowners have started coming to northern states to look for their runaways. It's not safe for you here," Harriet told her weary passengers.

A ND so she guided them farther north. She took them all the way to Canada. When they crossed the Canadian border, she turned to them with a smile.

"We've made it," she said. "You are safe, and you are free."

John threw his arms around her and hugged her. Eliza and Henry began singing with joy. All of them had tears running down their cheeks.

This was not Harriet's last trip on the Underground Railroad. She kept going back to help more runaways. In all, she led over 300 slaves to freedom. At the end of her career, she was able to say with pride, "No one ever caught me. And I never lost a single passenger."

WILLIAM AND ELLEN CRAFT
ESCAPE TO FREEDOM

When I was eleven years old, I was taken away from my mother. The master needed money, so he sold me. I can still remember the day my new master came and took me away. My mother followed the wagon for half a mile, crying and waving good-bye. It was the last time I ever saw her.

T HINK it over carefully, dear. What I am suggesting is terribly dangerous." William Craft spoke in a low voice to his wife Ellen as they sat in their slave cabin in Macon, Georgia.

"I understand," Ellen whispered. "And I know it's risky. But I am willing to risk everything to be free."

"You realize we might get caught," William continued in his deep, calm voice.

"Yes, I know that could happen."

"And you know that if we are caught, we will be punished. We might be sold to different masters. We might never see each other again. Our life together would be over. We are lucky now that our masters are neighbors and let us share this cabin. They even treat us well. If our plan fails, all that would change. No master can tolerate runaways."

Ellen said nothing for a moment. Then she took William's hand and looked into his eyes.

"I couldn't bear to be separated from you as I was from my mother. And I don't want that to happen to our children," she whispered. "Our children must not be born into slavery. We must try to reach the North and freedom."

William nodded. "Then we must make sure we succeed," he said firmly. "Your skin is light enough for you to pass as white, but I could never fool anyone. So you must pretend to be a white slaveowner on a journey to the North. I will be your personal slave."

"But no female slaveowner would have a man as a personal slave," Ellen pointed out.

"You're right," William agreed. "We must think of something else. Maybe if you dressed up as a man … yes. That way I could be your personal slave."

Ellen decided to wear a thick scarf around her face to hide her lack of whiskers. She would pretend to be suffering from a toothache. William was afraid her high, gentle voice would give her away. They decided she would pretend to be deaf and not talk to anyone.

"It will be perfect," William declared. "You will be a sickly old plantation owner, deaf and with a severe toothache. I will be your faithful servant taking you to a specialist up North."

They decided to leave on December 21, 1848. In the meantime, William counted and recounted his savings. Over the years his master had allowed him to build wooden cabinets in his spare time. He had sold these to local families for cash. He had saved enough money to buy train tickets to take them to the North and freedom.

AS December 21 approached, Ellen and William thought about nothing but their plan to escape. The details of it even began to invade their dreams. One night, Ellen awoke with a start.

"William!" she cried.

"What's the matter?" he asked, alarmed.

"I just realized. It will take us four or five days to reach Philadelphia. We'll have to stay in several hotels!"

"Don't worry," William assured her. "We have money for that."

"It's not the money," Ellen answered. "Think about it: I can't read or write. How can I sign the register books at the hotels?"

William sat up straight. This was a problem he

hadn't considered. As they discussed it, Ellen finally came up with an idea.

"I'll wrap my arm in a bandage and put it in a sling," Ellen stated. "You can tell people that I had a riding accident. Or better yet, just say I'm old and stiff and crippled."

At last the day arrived. As the sun rose over the trees, William and Ellen made their final preparations. Ellen dressed in men's clothing. William cut off all of her long black curls. Ellen put her right arm into a sling and wrapped a scarf about her face. Then they knelt together in the early morning light and prayed for safe passage.

AT the train station, Ellen boarded the car for white passengers. William went to ride in the car for blacks. Ellen sat nervously by the window as the train pulled out. Suddenly, she heard a familiar voice. Turning around, she saw Mr. Cray, an old friend of her master's. He was walking straight toward her! Fear pierced Ellen's heart. This man had known her for years. He had spoken with her just yesterday when he visited her master's farm for dinner.

Her heart pounding, Ellen turned away and stared out the window. When Mr. Cray reached

her seat, he sat down next to her. Ellen grew dizzy with fright. She struggled to calm herself. After a few moments, however, she realized that Mr. Cray didn't recognize her. He thought that she was just a fellow passenger.

Slowly she began to relax. But then Mr. Cray turned to her and began talking.

"It is a very fine morning, sir," he said to her.

Ellen could not keep her palms from sweating. She knew she could not have a conversation with this man. Her voice would surely give her away. She did not respond to his comment, but kept looking out the window.

"I said, it is a very fine morning, sir," Mr. Cray said again.

Ellen could see that he was becoming annoyed. When he repeated his remark a third time in a louder voice, she knew she had no choice. She bowed her head and turned toward him.

"Yes," she said gruffly.

Then she turned away again. For a moment Mr. Cray said nothing. Terrified, Ellen held her breath. She expected Mr. Cray to jump up and call for the porter. She was sure she was going to be arrested. He must have recognized her in spite of her disguise. But after a long minute, she heard him sigh and settle back in his seat.

"How difficult it must be to be deaf," he mumbled to himself. "I shall not trouble that poor old fellow anymore."

For the rest of the journey, Mr. Cray did not say a word to Ellen. Still, she remained tense and frightened. When the train pulled into Savannah, Georgia, she felt tremendously relieved. They had completed the first part of their trip!

IN Savannah, Ellen bought two boat tickets to Charleston, South Carolina. From Charleston, she and William would take a series of trains north toward Philadelphia.

The trip north progressed without incident until they reached Baltimore, Maryland. This was their last stop before reaching the free state of Pennsylvania. When they tried to board the train bound for Philadelphia, the ticket master stopped them.

"Wait one moment!" he said to Ellen. "I want to see proof that you own this slave."

Ellen didn't know what to do. She tried to remain calm. They had come so far without a problem! Now she could only fumble around as though looking for something. Meanwhile, William's mind was racing. As Ellen pretended to sift through her pockets, he spoke up.

"Excuse me, sir, my master isn't well. I've got to get him to Philadelphia to see his doctor. He's been getting worse every day of this trip. I'm afraid he won't last much longer without the proper medicine. You must let him get on this train!"

The ticket master glared at William.

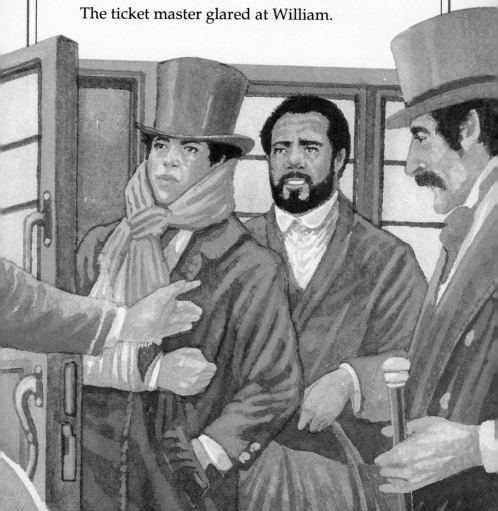

"No one gets on this train until I say so," he replied coldly. "Tell your master that I need to see the papers."

"I don't know anything about any papers, sir. I just know my master has got to get on this train!"

The ticket master turned to call a guard. A cry of despair caught in William's throat. Is this how their trip would end? After coming so close to freedom, would they be found out now and sent back to Georgia?

At that moment, however, a white man stepped up to the ticket master.

"Pardon me," the stranger said. "I couldn't help overhearing your conversation. I beg you to take pity on this poor man. Look at the gentleman. Clearly he is ill, perhaps even dying. Do not trouble him about the papers."

Several other people standing in line behind William spoke up in agreement.

"Yes," said one man. "The gentleman seems quite confused. Why don't you just let him board?"

"He's obviously ill," a woman chimed in. "Do not keep him any longer. Let his slave help him to his seat."

In the face of these outbursts, the ticket master seemed confused and embarrassed.

"Certainly I didn't mean to upset the gentleman," he said to the group. "Go ahead, sir. And next time bring your papers." With that, he stepped aside and motioned for William and Ellen to board the train.

TREMBLING with relief, they stepped aboard. William helped Ellen to her seat, then he went to sit in the car marked "Blacks Only." Several hours later, the train pulled into the Philadelphia station. Weak from frayed nerves and tired from lack of sleep, William and Ellen staggered onto the platform. As they stepped onto the free soil of Philadelphia, they forgot their weariness. Joyously, they took deep breaths of the clean, cold air of freedom.

"We did it, William, we did it!" Ellen cried. "We're free!"

Arm in arm, William and Ellen Craft walked out of the train station to begin their new life as free people.

Angelina and Sarah Grimké

Sisters Against Slavery

I live in a huge mansion. Fields stretch for miles around, rich with crops. Each day, these fields are tended carefully, season after season. The money from the crops gives my family a life of luxury.

But I am not a happy and contented Southern belle. Underneath, I am an angry woman!

I'M sorry, Mother," Angelina Grimké said firmly. "I just cannot stay here any longer."

"But Angelina, how can you leave? Think of what you are giving up!" Mrs. Grimké stood on the porch of her beautiful South Carolina home, pleading with her 24-year-old daughter. "I'm sure we can work something out. Please — let's sit down and talk this over."

But Angelina was in no mood to talk. She was ready for action.

"We've been through all this before, Mother. You and Father are slaveowners. I look around this house and I see black women doing the housework. I look outside and I see the men doing backbreaking farm work from sunup to sundown. You treat them like machines — but they're not! They're people, and they deserve to have a life, just as you and I do. Do we live just to work? No! — I can't live here anymore. You can look at all this and not feel bad, but I can't. I can no longer live in a house that abides slavery!"

Angelina headed for her room to pack her bags. She wanted to move far from her life of luxury. Her family's beautiful gardens, fancy parties, and life of ease filled her with anger. She knew the Grimké way of life depended on the use of slaves, and she wanted no part of it.

"I'll join my sister Sarah in Philadelphia," she thought to herself. "Life there will be different. I won't have to be a part of all this."

After a tense farewell, Angelina left her parents' home. She took a train from Charleston, South Carolina and arrived in Philadelphia in the hot summer of 1829. Exhausted but excited, she spotted her older sister on the platform waving to her.

"Sarah!" cried Angelina.

"You made it!" exclaimed Sarah, rushing to greet her. "I'm so glad you're here. I've missed you."

"Yes," said Angelina, "I've missed you, too. I'm so glad to be here. It will be wonderful to live where people don't believe in slavery. It was terrible back in Charleston. I couldn't remain there surrounded by slaveowners."

"Well, all that's behind you now," said Sarah happily. "Here you won't have to think about slavery at all."

Angelina stopped suddenly and looked at her sister. Something about those last words made her uncomfortable.

"Is that what I am doing?" Angelina asked herself. "Have I moved here so that I won't have to think about the slaves? Will I be able to forget about them?"

Sarah noticed the strange, serious look on Angelina's face. "What's the matter, Angelina?" she asked.

"Oh, nothing," Angelina replied absently, "I was just thinking … "

AFTER settling in Philadelphia, Angelina joined the Quakers. Sarah had been a member for several years, and Angelina found the Quaker outlook appealing. Quakers lived simple lives. They dressed in plain clothes and held weekly meetings to talk about their faith. Best of all, they stood firmly opposed to slavery.

Angelina also began reading *The Liberator*, an antislavery newspaper. In 1835, Angelina wrote a letter to *The Liberator*. Her letter described how unjust slavery was. It also condemned anyone who tolerated slavery, especially church members. When *The Liberator* printed the entire letter, some of Angelina's fellow Quakers were furious.

"You had no right to send that letter to *The Liberator*," stated one Quaker. "It is against the rules of the Society to publish anything until the elders read it and approve it."

Even Sarah thought Angelina had been rash. "You must apologize right away," she urged.

Angelina ignored these comments. She felt more content than she had ever felt before.

"At last I am standing up for what I really believe," she told Sarah. "You should do the same."

THE next year, Angelina wrote a 36-page pamphlet, which she called "An Appeal to the Christian Women of the South." In it, she urged women to rise up and demand an end to slavery. Members of the American Antislavery Society printed thousands of these pamphlets. Then they mailed them to people in the southern states.

Landowners in the South were furious. Post office officials refused to deliver the pamphlets.

They held public gatherings to burn them. The mayor of Charleston, South Carolina, grimly announced that Angelina Grimké was no longer welcome in her hometown.

"If she tries to come back here, she will be arrested and thrown in prison," he warned.

Angelina had no intention of going back. She did not want to return to her past. She wanted to forge ahead and find new ways to express her beliefs. Soon she had the perfect opportunity to voice her opinions. The Antislavery Society invited her to New York to give a speech.

"You're not going to do it, are you?" Sarah asked fearfully.

"Why not?" asked Angelina.

"Angelina! You've never spoken in public. You're so shy you never even talk during the meeting of Friends! Certainly some people won't agree with you. What will you do then? Besides, women don't speak in public. It isn't proper."

"Isn't proper?" Angelina said heatedly. "I will tell you what isn't proper. It isn't proper for any people to put chains on the ankles of other people.

It isn't proper for any group to sell others for work, the way they would sell a machine or an animal. No one can own another person!"

"Well — you're right — but — " Sarah struggled for other reasons to give Angelina. Even as she did, she had the nagging feeling that she was wrong and Angelina was right.

"Well, what about the Quakers?" she said at last. "They could disown you for stirring up trouble."

"Yes, they could," Angelina admitted. "That would make me sad. But I would be more miserable if I ignored my own conscience and didn't do what I believe to be right."

"Well, what about your safety? If you speak out against slavery, someone might try to hurt you. You'd be risking your life!"

Angelina looked directly into her sister's eyes. "Is my life more important than the life of a slave?" she asked.

This time Sarah had no reply. She had run out of arguments.

"Very well. I'll come with you and give a speech, too," Sarah burst out suddenly.

"Are you serious?" Angelina asked in surprise.

"Yes, I am. It is time that I, too, began to follow my conscience."

IN November 1836, the Grimké sisters traveled to New York. There they met Theodore Weld, a well-known member of the Antislavery Society. He escorted them to the place where they were scheduled to speak.

"I hope you are prepared for some hostile listeners," he said.

"But I thought most people in New York opposed slavery," said Angelina.

"That's not the problem. The problem is that many people in New York think that women should *not* give public lectures. Threatening letters have been pouring in to our office all week. Today, leaflets are being passed around urging people to come and 'teach those Grimké women a lesson.'"

Sarah shuddered, but Angelina spoke calmly. "That's all right," she said. "I'm not afraid. Justice is on my side."

WHEN they arrived, the sisters found 300 people waiting to hear them. Angelina walked to the front to begin her speech. She looked out at the sea of people. A few faces were friendly. But most stared at her disapprovingly. Many people had come just out of curiosity. Suddenly, a wave of terror rushed over her. Her face turned deathly white. Words flew out of her head, and she stood speechless before the crowd.

As Sarah watched in dismay, Angelina closed her eyes and said a short prayer. She prayed for the courage to speak the truth. When she opened her eyes, she felt better.

"I have something important to say," she thought. "And this is my chance to say it."

Slowly she began to speak. "I have seen slavery," she told the assembled people. "My family and I have been slaveowners. I am here to tell you that slavery is wrong."

As Angelina spoke, her confidence grew. Her voice became clear and strong. People sat on the edge of their seats, listening intently. When Angelina finished, Sarah stood up. Although Sarah was not as strong a speaker, she, too, had important things to say. Her honesty and sincerity swept over the audience with great force. When she finished, the listeners jumped up, clapping wildly. The Grimké sisters had made everyone present feel the burning injustice of slavery.

Angelina and Sarah went on to give many more speeches. For fifteen months they toured New England. They spoke to larger and larger groups of Northerners. They helped found the first Female Antislavery Society in America. They even spoke to the Massachusetts legislature, a first for women. They retired from public life in 1838, but their actions remained a powerful example to women everywhere. In helping to light the fire of freedom for others, the Grimké sisters also ignited a spark for the independence of women in America.

LORENZO DE ZAVALA

THE STRUGGLE FOR DEMOCRACY

Emily, I really don't want to leave Mexico. This is the land of my birth. I have devoted my life to helping the people of my country. I have poured my energy into this new government. Finally, Mexico can become a land of freedom and opportunity for all.

But now I'm called away to France. I hope that nothing goes wrong while we're away. The future of Mexico is in the hands of President Santa Anna.

I knew it!" cried Lorenzo de Zavala bitterly. "I knew Santa Anna was becoming hungry for power. I helped elect him president of Mexico. And now look! He has proclaimed himself dictator! He has ignored the Constitution of 1824! Mexico has lost its chance for a free government."

De Zavala shook with anger. He had devoted himself to making Mexico a democracy. He was serving his country as minister to France. But while de Zavala was in France, Santa Anna had taken over Mexico's government completely.

De Zavala wrote a long letter to Santa Anna. He accused him of destroying the liberty guaranteed in the Mexican Constitution. De Zavala also resigned as foreign minister.

"What will we do now?" cried his wife, Emily, in dismay. "After you send that letter, we can never return to Mexico. Santa Anna would have you put in jail." Emily began to cry. "Where will we go now? Will we have to stay in France forever?"

"No," declared de Zavala. He thought for a few minutes. Then he announced, "We will go to Texas."

"What good will that do? Texas is part of Mexico! Our lives will still be in danger," said Emily in confusion.

"Yes, it is part of Mexico," de Zavala conceded. "But most Texans are settlers who came from the United States, not Mexico. They understand the values of liberty and freedom. They will not sit still while Santa Anna forces them to accept his will. When they hear what he is doing, they will rise up and overthrow Santa Anna."

"How can you be so sure?" Emily persisted.

"Believe me," said de Zavala firmly. "The people of Texas will not give up their freedom without a fight."

Soon after this, the de Zavalas sailed for America. After arriving in New York, they made their way to New Orleans and then to Texas. It was a difficult time for de Zavala. He felt betrayed by Santa Anna, and he worried about Mexico's future. He had trouble sleeping and spent many restless nights. By the time they arrived in Texas in July 1835, de Zavala's health was poor. He suffered from chills and fevers that came and went without warning.

IN Texas, de Zavala picked out a homesite on the banks of Buffalo Bayou, near the San Jacinto River. He went to work warning Texans about the power-hungry Santa Anna.

"Must you leave again?" Emily asked him one morning in August 1835. "Every day you ride off to a new settlement to talk to the people. You

should rest. Your health will not last if you keep driving yourself this hard."

De Zavala kissed Emily's cheek. "I will rest soon," he promised. "As soon as Santa Anna is no longer the leader of Mexico."

With that, de Zavala rode into downtown Harrisburg (now Houston) to address the people there. As he rode, he thought about Emily's words. She was right. He was working too hard. He was sacrificing his health.

"But it's a sacrifice I must make," he told himself. "I must spread the word about Santa Anna."

In Harrisburg, de Zavala found many citizens gathered in a blacksmith shop in the center of town. He spoke to them about the crisis that all Texans faced.

"Santa Anna is a dictator. He wants to control everything in Mexico and Texas. Even though Texas is many miles from the capital of Mexico, Santa Anna will still try to control our land. He will not stop unless we stop him!"

A man in the crowd spoke up. "Some of us have been talking about Santa Anna for days," said the man, whose name was John Wharton. "And we think we should break away from Mexico altogether. We no longer have any rights, and the Mexican government won't listen to us."

Startled, de Zavala paused. He hadn't considered this idea before. "You mean you want to declare Texas an independent country?" he asked slowly.

"Yes!" shouted Wharton.

"That's right!" echoed several others. "We'll form a Republic of Texas — our own country!"

De Zavala remained silent. He wanted time to think about this bold new proposal. He excused himself from the group and started for home.

As he rode along, de Zavala thought about Texas becoming independent. In some ways, this new idea made sense. Most Texans had a different cultural background than other Mexican citizens. Besides, Texans wanted a free democratic government, and they were not likely to get it from Mexico.

"Yes," he thought at last. "I will support the fight for Texas independence. Texas should be a country of its own."

True to his belief, de Zavala threw his efforts into helping the newly formed "War Party" achieve independence for Texas.

I N October, de Zavala planned to appear at a special meeting of Texans to talk about their future. His experience and knowledge of government affairs would help the Texans. On the day of the meeting, however, he became ill. From his sickbed he wrote a letter to be read at the meeting. In it he outlined the dangers of Santa Anna's rule and called on Texans to stand up and fight against the dictator.

He was still in bed a few days later when Emily rushed in with a worried look on her face.

"John Wharton just stopped by on his way to Harrisburg," she said. "Something incredible has happened."

"What?" asked de Zavala.

"Santa Anna has issued a demand for your arrest. If the Texans do not turn you over to the Mexican army, Santa Anna is threatening to march north and attack the Texas settlers."

De Zavala swallowed hard. "What did Wharton say?" he asked. "Will they turn me in?"

"No," Emily said, her head held high. "They called a special meeting. Then they issued this statement: 'We will not give up any individual to the military authorities of Mexico.' Isn't that wonderful, Lorenzo? They are all standing behind you."

De Zavala nodded and smiled with relief. "I must hurry and get well," he said, "so I can help the people of Texas win their freedom."

By winter de Zavala felt much better. As he resumed his meetings with other Texas leaders, he knew that Santa Anna was growing impatient. He was sure that full-scale war would soon break out.

IN March 1836, Texans held a convention at Washington-on-the-Brazos. De Zavala attended the meeting as a delegate from Harrisburg. His knowledge of government helped the delegates reach a final decision. On March 2, 1836, these leaders declared Texas independent from Mexican rule! They knew there was no turning back after such a declaration. Santa Anna would not accept their action without a fight.

"Now," said de Zavala, "we must build a new government that is just and fair and free. Until elections can be held, we need a temporary government."

For two weeks the delegates worked on a plan of government. But then, on March 16, they received the news they had dreaded. Santa Anna and his army were on the march. They had massacred everyone at the Alamo on March 6 and were heading toward Washington-on-the-Brazos.

"He's after me," said de Zavala grimly when he heard the news.

"What?" asked a fellow delegate.

"Santa Anna. He's after me. That's why he's in such a hurry. He wants to crush the new Texas republic, but he also wants to crush me. He calls me a traitor to my country."

The delegates showed their support of de Zavala by electing him the temporary Vice President of the Republic of Texas on March 17. Then the convention quickly adjourned. In a pouring rain, de Zavala and the other officials of the new country retreated to Harrisburg.

N March 23, de Zavala returned home to see his family.

"Lorenzo!" cried Emily joyfully when she saw her husband approaching. "I'm so glad to see you. I've been so worried."

De Zavala took Emily in his arms and told her all that had happened in the three weeks he had been away. Then he went into his cabin and hugged his three children.

"We must be ready to leave at a moment's notice," he warned Emily that night.

"What do you mean?" she asked, frightened.

"Santa Anna and his army are moving in this direction. We must not let them catch us."

On April 15, de Zavala sensed danger moving closer. At noon that day he and his family left for the safety of Galveston Island. Later the same day, Santa Anna rode into Harrisburg. He burned the town, then went to an area near the San Jacinto River to make camp. The campsite was close to de Zavala's home.

The next day, while Santa Anna and his army rested from their march, Texas troops led by Sam Houston made a surprise attack on Santa Anna's army. In a battle that lasted only eighteen minutes, the Texans completely destroyed Santa Anna's forces. Santa Anna was taken prisoner.

When de Zavala heard this news, he was overjoyed. At last, his dream of living in a democratic republic had come true. In a democracy, the people would *elect* government leaders to make laws for them. Never had de Zavala felt so free. As he looked back over the years, he had no regrets. He was proud of his Mexican heritage, and he was equally proud to be a founder of the Republic of Texas.

WILLIAM TRAVIS

DEFENDER OF THE ALAMO

Dear Charles,

You are only six years old, so this may be hard for you to understand. I am here at the Alamo, defending it against the Mexican army. I'm doing this for you, Charles, and for all people who want to be free. I may not see you again, so I want you to know I love you very much.

Your father,

William B. Travis

COLONEL William B. Travis peered over the wall of the old mission called the Alamo. Across the river, in the town of San Antonio, Texas, a bright red flag waved from a church tower. As it fluttered in the breeze, William Travis took a slow, deep breath.

"The Mexican army has raised the red flag," he announced to his friend Davy Crockett.

Crockett did not answer. He merely tightened his grip on "Old Betsy," the rifle that he always carried with him, and straightened his coonskin cap. Both he and Travis knew what the red flag meant: the Mexican army would take no prisoners. If the Texans lost the battle, they would all be killed.

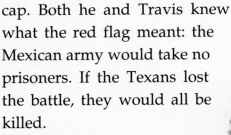

That night, the 26-year-old Travis paced back and forth through the courtyard of the

Alamo. Beside him walked Davy Crockett, who at the age of 49 still had the energy and vigor of a young man.

"Maybe I should have surrendered when I had the chance," Travis said to Crockett. "After all, we have less than two hundred men. General Santa Anna has over a thousand. He has us surrounded, and now he's just waiting for his extra troops to arrive. When they do come, he'll surely attack. Unless we get help soon, we don't stand a chance."

"You did the right thing," Crockett reassured him. "Santa Anna asked you to give up without a fight. You couldn't do that. There is honor in winning and honor in losing. But there is no honor in surrendering."

Travis looked at Crockett and smiled a sad smile. "I know," he said softly. "Still … " As his voice trailed off, he thought of the days ahead. He knew that Santa Anna was hungry for a victory. The Mexican General wanted to capture the Alamo. He wanted to prove that Texas was still under Mexican control. Texans, on the other hand, were fighting for their independence. They wanted Texas to be a country independent of Mexico. Travis knew that the conflict would end in death for both sides.

"I wonder if I'll ever see my son Charles again. I wonder if any of us will see our loved ones, if we will ever get out of here ..." he thought to himself. His heart ached as he thought about his six-year-old son and the brave men under his command.

"Come on now, Travis," Crockett said at last. "That's enough thinking for one night. Let's do what we can to cheer up the men."

Reminded of his duty, Travis shook off his sad thoughts.

"You're right," he said. "Why don't you get your fiddle? Where's McGregor with his bagpipes? Let's have some music!"

THE next day, February 24, 1836, Travis sat down in the old chapel of the Alamo. Taking out a pen and paper, he wrote the following message.

To the people of Texas and all Americans,
I am besieged by a thousand or more of the Mexicans under Santa Anna. The enemy has demanded our surrender, but our flag still waves proudly from the walls. *I shall never surrender or retreat.* I call on you in the name of liberty and patriotism to come to our aid. If this call is neglected, I am determined to sustain myself as long as possible and die

like a soldier who never forgets what is due to his own honor and that of his country: VICTORY OR DEATH.

After signing this letter, Travis sent for a messenger to carry it past enemy lines. Then he walked outside and called to his men.

"Men," he declared, "I am sure that help will arrive soon. Texans will heed our call for reinforcements. Until that time, let's show the enemy what we can do. Let's show 'em how Texans can fight to gain independence!"

The next day, one of the lookouts shouted an alarm. Travis rushed to the top of the wall. He saw a group of Mexican soldiers charging toward the Alamo.

"There aren't many troops. It must be an advance unit to test our strength," Travis said.

He gave an order, and the Alamo's cannons shot out a series of explosive balls. In the face of these deadly blows, the enemy soon turned back.

"Well," said Travis, wiping the sweat from his forehead, "we've won the first round. I hope the next round proves to be as easy."

THE next round came two days later. On February 27, the Mexicans began a furious bombardment of the mission. Travis ordered his men to return the attack with rifle fire and cannonballs. For the next few days, nothing changed. The two sides continued to exchange shots. The Mexicans couldn't get past the Texas gunfire. But they never stopped trying. Santa Anna sent wave after wave of soldiers toward the mission.

Meanwhile, Travis's hopes of getting fresh troops grew dimmer and dimmer.

"Even if some men are on their way, they probably won't get here in time," he thought bleakly.

On March 3, things got worse. That day one of Travis's scouts returned from San Antonio with bad news.

"Santa Anna's reinforcements have arrived!" he cried. "There are thousands of them. Thousands!"

This was what Travis had feared most. Now Santa Anna would be free to launch an all-out attack against the Alamo. With fewer than two hundred men, Travis knew he couldn't hold off the enemy for very long. The Alamo would almost certainly fall to Santa Anna's forces.

A dozen thoughts raced through Travis's head.

He thought of his law career, his son, his hopes for the future. He thought of trying to make a last-minute escape under the cover of darkness. Then he thought of Texas. He thought of the cause of liberty and independence from Mexico. He thought of freedom and honor and his duty to his country. He knew he could not run away. He must stay to face the enemy. He would sacrifice his life for Texas.

Taking out a scrap of paper, Travis wrote a quick note to David Ayres, the man who looked after his son.

"Take care of my little boy," Travis wrote as tears filled his eyes. "If the country should be saved, I may make him a splendid fortune. But if the country should be lost, he will have nothing but the proud memory that he is the son of a man who died for his country."

THAT night Travis walked boldly out into the courtyard. He called to all the men to gather there. Then in a firm, clear voice, he explained the situation.

"Santa Anna's reinforcements have arrived," he announced. "Full-scale battle will break out very soon. I'm going to give each of you a choice. If you wish, you can slip out of the Alamo right now. It is dark, and you can probably get through the Mexican lines. Or you can stay here with me and fight. If you stay, you must know that you will probably die. But remember, you will be dying for a noble cause. You will be dying for the cause of freedom. Your lives will help win independence for Texas."

Silence filled the courtyard. William Travis looked at each of his men. Then he pulled out his sword and drew a line in the dirt.

"Everyone who chooses to stay and fight should cross this line to join me."

Davy Crockett stepped across the line, looked his friend in the eye, and gave him a proud salute. The others followed. One man, Jim Bowie, was ill and could not walk. Bowie asked his fellow Texans to carry him across the line.

Soon all but one man stood next to Travis. This man, Louis Rose, was a soldier of fortune. He would fight for money, but he cared nothing for Texas independence.

"Come stand with us," urged Jim Bowie.

But Rose did not move.

"Let him go," Travis commanded.

Rose did not wait for another word. He ran to the wall and climbed up. Then he jumped down onto the other side.

After he had gone, the rest of the men settled down to wait for Santa Anna's attack. It came on March 6, thirteen days after the siege had begun. At five o'clock in the morning, a blast from a Mexican bugle cut through the chilly Texas air. This was the signal that the attack was beginning.

As Mexican soldiers charged the Alamo from all sides, Travis and his men stood ready.

The Alamo's cannons and rifles tore into the Mexican ranks, killing and wounding many. Again and again, the Mexicans had to retreat and regroup.

FINALLY, Santa Anna called upon his reserve troops. This time their massive assault broke through the Alamo's north wall. Hundreds of Mexican soldiers poured through the opening and attacked the Texans.

"Don't give up, men! Keep fighting!" Travis yelled as he turned to confront the enemy inside the courtyard. But just as he pulled out his sword to fend off an attacker, a Mexican soldier took aim and fired. A single bullet struck Travis and killed him.

Meanwhile, the other Texans began fighting hand-to-hand. With Mexicans swarming into the fort, they didn't have time to reload their guns. They fought courageously. Even the ailing Jim Bowie fought bravely from his cot. In the end, though, there was no hope. Santa Anna had too many soldiers. When the smoke finally cleared, all the defenders of the Alamo lay dead. Over 1,000 Mexican soldiers had also died.

In making their last stand, William B. Travis and his men gave up their lives. But their bravery and heroism inspired thousands of others across Texas. As word of the battle spread, Texans shouted a new rallying cry: "Remember the Alamo!"

ELIZABETH CADY STANTON

THE MOTHER OF EQUALITY
FOR WOMEN

Elizabeth, I agreed that our marriage vows need not include the word "obey." I realize that equality is important to you. But you are going too far now. You are suggesting — no, demanding too much when you ask that women be allowed to vote.

ELEVEN-year-old Elizabeth Cady sat in the corner of her father's chambers. She loved being here. She loved the musty smell of the law books and leather-covered chairs. Most of all, she loved watching her father work. On this wintry day in 1826, he planned to meet with some poor local residents who sought his advice. As long as Elizabeth sat quietly, he had agreed to let her stay and listen.

The first person to come in was a middle-aged woman. Tears ran down her cheeks.

"Judge Cady," the woman said, "thank you so much for seeing me. I didn't know where else to turn. You see, my husband died on Friday. Pneumonia, the doctor said. Yesterday I began looking through his personal papers. And this is what I found."

Choking back a sob, the woman handed Judge Cady a wrinkled piece of paper. Elizabeth leaned forward in her chair, trying to see what was written on the paper.

"It's his will," the woman explained. "It says that all the property now belongs to our oldest son, Jacob."

"I see," said Judge Cady soberly.

"Well, sir, that can't be right. Most of the money left is money *I* earned as a washerwoman. How

could my husband give away money I earned? How could he give away my home and my belongings? Surely the law won't permit such a thing!"

Elizabeth looked at her father with trusting eyes. She knew that he would fix things. After all, he was a judge. Wasn't it a judge's job to make sure that justice was done?

But to her dismay, Judge Cady simply shook his head. "I'm sorry," he said. "There's nothing I can do."

Elizabeth jumped up from her chair. She could not believe what she had heard.

"Father!" she cried. "How can you say that? Why can't you help this woman?"

Judge Cady looked at Elizabeth with stern but sympathetic eyes. "I know it seems unjust," he said quietly, speaking both to Elizabeth and to the woman, "but according to the law, married women cannot own property. Everything they have belongs to their husbands. And men are free to manage their property as they choose. It may not be fair, but it's the law."

Elizabeth felt as if her whole world had been shaken. She felt weak and angry. How could such a law exist? How could people accept this unfair law?

"If the law doesn't treat women fairly," she fumed, "then the law should be changed! And when I grow up, I'm going to change it!"

As Elizabeth grew older, she observed many more things that disturbed her. She learned that women could not attend the same colleges as men. They could not become lawyers, physicians, or politicians. If women did work as teachers, seamstresses, or housekeepers, they had no control over the money they earned. Their wages went to their fathers or their husbands. Most importantly, women did not have the right to vote. And without the right to vote, women could not hope to change the laws that worked against them.

I N 1833, when Elizabeth was 18, she became involved in the growing antislavery movement. Her cousin, Gerrit Smith, was an active abolitionist. He ran a station on the Underground Railroad in Peterboro, New York. Elizabeth saw runaway slaves helped to freedom and witnessed the courage of those who helped them.

Elizabeth decided to help free the slaves. She hoped her work might lead to more rights for women, too. Both women and slaves were denied certain basic rights, such as the right to own property, manage their own money, and vote.

At one antislavery meeting, Elizabeth met a young man named Henry B. Stanton. The two soon fell in love and became engaged. As they planned the wedding, Elizabeth expressed her dislike for traditional wedding vows.

"What do you mean?" Henry asked, bewildered.

"I won't promise to 'love, honor, and obey' you. I love you, and I will honor you, but I will not obey you. 'Obey' implies that the wife is less than her husband. Ours must be a marriage of equals."

Henry smiled. "I understand," he said. "We'll tell the minister to leave that word out of the ceremony."

Elizabeth beamed. She felt very lucky to have found someone who shared and respected her beliefs.

IN May of 1840, Elizabeth and Henry were married. They moved to Seneca Falls, New York, and had several children. Elizabeth still participated in many antislavery rallies. In July 1848, she began to make plans for a new kind of convention.

"It will be the first convention ever to focus on women's rights," she told Henry excitedly. "It's going to convene right here in Seneca Falls, at the

Wesleyan Methodist Church. I've contacted Lucretia Mott, and she has agreed to come. When word gets out that the greatest female abolitionist of our time will be there, I'm sure lots of people will want to attend."

Henry squeezed Elizabeth's hand. "I'm proud of you," he said, "proud to see you putting your beliefs into action."

With the convention drawing near, Elizabeth went to work on a statement. She called it the Declaration of Sentiments. She wanted participants at the conference to adopt her declaration of women's rights.

"I've patterned it after the Declaration of Independence," she told Henry. "I'm going to read it at the convention. It discusses the low status of women in this country. And it includes a list of twelve proposed changes in the present law."

"What a good idea!" Henry said. "What specific changes do you call for?"

"Well," said Elizabeth, "the most important one is suffrage. Women *must* be given the right to vote."

Henry looked at Elizabeth with worried eyes. "Surely you won't include voting rights in your resolutions," he exclaimed in shock. "It's too radical! You will upset the whole convention. No one will take the other recommendations seriously."

"But women will never have true political power until they have the right to vote," Elizabeth replied quietly.

"Well," said Henry stubbornly, "I cannot support your resolution. If you go ahead with this recommendation, I will not set foot in the church. I will have nothing to do with the convention."

Elizabeth fought back tears. She had not expected opposition from Henry on this important point. Sadly, she folded up her Declaration of Sentiments. She said nothing more to her husband about the convention.

WHEN Lucretia Mott arrived, Elizabeth told her about the Declaration of Sentiments and her resolution for women's voting rights. She felt sure that Mrs. Mott would support her ideas. Again, she was wrong.

"Nobody will support suffrage!" Mrs. Mott protested. "And, no one will support a convention that calls for such an impossible task. We should concentrate on smaller, more attainable goals."

Elizabeth was crushed. She had no idea she would have so much opposition.

On the day before the convention, Elizabeth stood outside the church. Staring at the majestic building in front of her, she focused on the problems she faced.

"If I include the resolution, I risk embarrassment and defeat. I might doom this convention to failure even before it starts. But winning the right to vote is important to me. It is something I have wanted to propose since I realized that voting is the key to fair laws."

Elizabeth stared up at the church steeple standing bright against the blue sky. She wrestled with her decision for a long time.

"I hope that I am not making a mistake," she thought at last, "but I must proclaim my beliefs. If I don't have the courage to stand up for what I believe, I don't deserve the right to vote."

THE next day, Elizabeth marched into the crowded church. She read aloud her Declaration of Sentiments, including the resolution about women's right to vote.

Immediately, voices shouted out in protest. Elizabeth resolutely began to answer each one. As she spoke, she spotted Frederick Douglass sitting in the audience. Turning to the famous ex-slave, she asked for his help.

"Mr. Douglass," she cried, "you, like myself, are not allowed to vote. You must see that the root of our legal problems lies in the fact that we cannot make laws for ourselves. Surely you, of all people, understand the importance of the vote."

The distinguished Mr. Douglass rose to his feet. "Yes," he called out, "I support your resolution."

Elizabeth and Mr. Douglass spoke eloquently in favor of women's right to vote. After two days of discussion, the convention finally voted to adopt the entire Declaration of Sentiments.

Elizabeth was thrilled. She had done it! She had taken the first step toward changing the legal status of women in America. She felt certain that her Seneca Falls convention would make history. For the first time on record, people had stood up and spoken out in favor of women's rights, including the right to vote.

As news of the convention spread, people began to rethink their attitudes about women. Many came to understand and support Elizabeth's position. Although women did not gain the right to vote until 1920, 72 years after Elizabeth's convention, she had started a movement that would change forever the status of women in society.

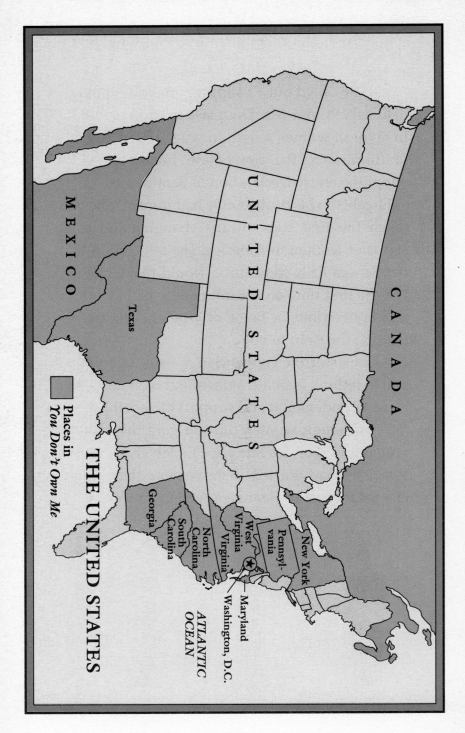

THE UNITED STATES

Places in
You Don't Own Me

MEXICO

UNITED STATES

CANADA

Texas

Georgia

South
Carolina

North
Carolina

Virginia

West
Virginia

Pennsyl-
vania

New York

Maryland

Washington, D.C.

ATLANTIC
OCEAN